OVER

UNDER

Which animal is going
to win the race?

FAST

Can you spot the
hidden mouse?

FINISH

At home

DAY

What animal is asleep during the day?

AWAKE

OPEN

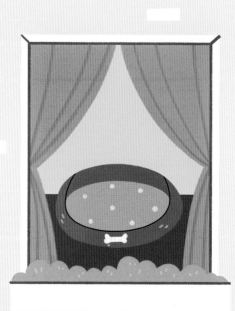

LIGHT

In the jungle

LAZY

ACTIVE

How many butterflies can you count?

PATTERNED

PLAIN

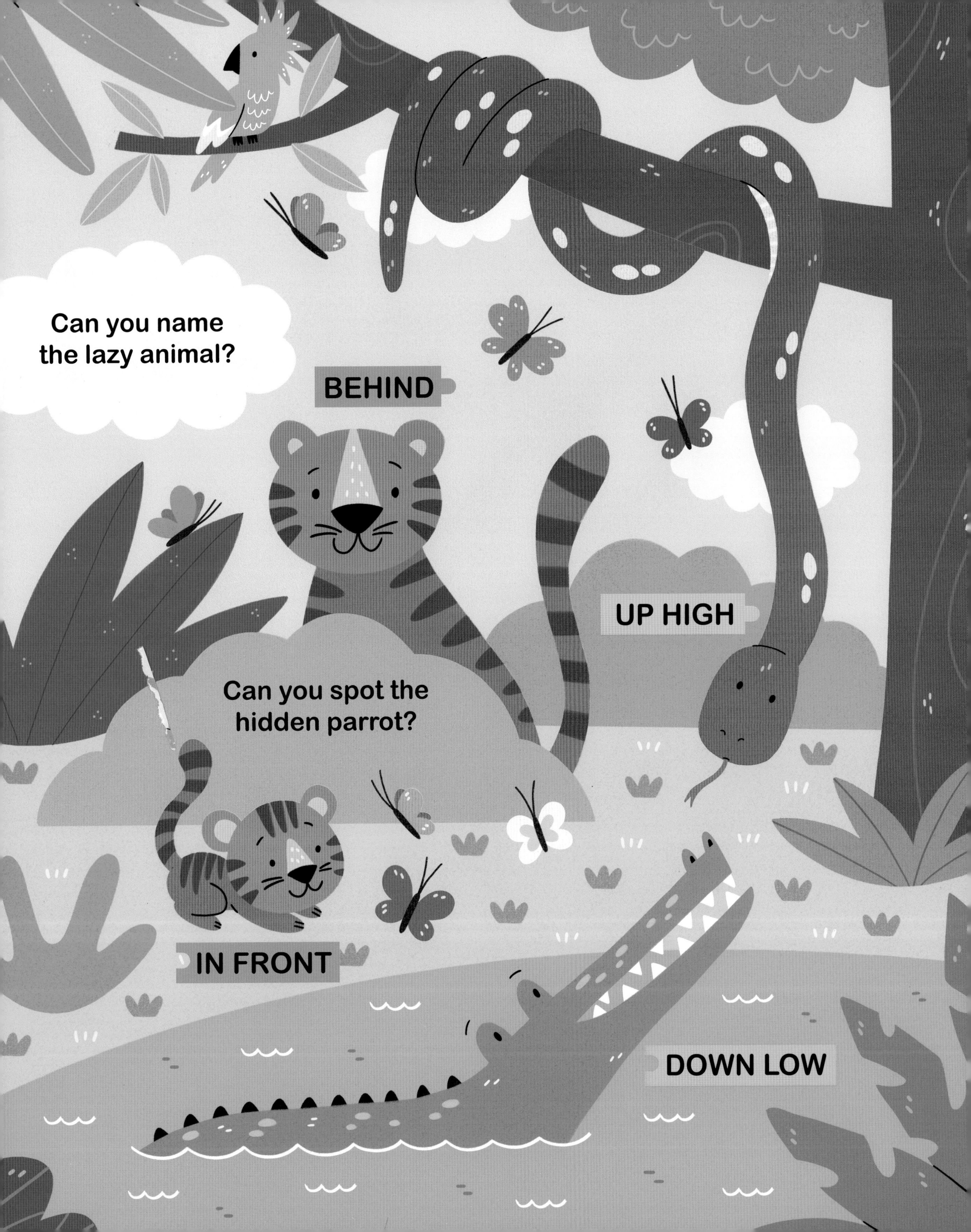
Can you name the lazy animal?
BEHIND
UP HIGH
Can you spot the hidden parrot?
IN FRONT
DOWN LOW

On the road

Can you spot the hidden cat?

GO

How many people are on the bus?

WAIT

LAST

FIRST

STANDING SITTING

STOP

LEFT

RIGHT

What does the green traffic light mean?

OLD YOUNG

At the playground

TOP

SHORT

TALL

Can you spot the hidden rabbit?

BOTTOM

Can you spot the difference between the two rockets?

On the farm

Follow the path to lead the sheep back to its family.

MANY

INSIDE

OUTSIDE

DIRTY   CLEAN

FEW

How many carrots
can you count?

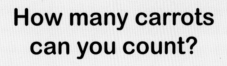

FULL

EMPTY

Which cow is the
odd one out?

In summer

FAR

How many shells
can you count?

WET

DRY

NEAR

What food
do you have at
the beach?

At the shop

What are two differences between the trains?

NEW

OLD

GIVE

TAKE

Puzzle time

Can you match
each big puzzle piece
to its opposite?

RIGHT

SOFT

FAST

HAPPY

HEAVY

SICK